Visions from My Heart

A COLLECTION OF POEMS BY
TRAVIS WOODS

Visions from My Heart

Copyright © 2022,
Travis Woods, Author

Contact the Author: **tw031954@gmail.com**

Kingdom News Publication Services, LLC., Publisher

DISCLAIMER

All the material contained in this book is provided for educational and informational purposes only. No responsibility can be taken for any results or outcomes resulting from the use of this material.

While every attempt has been made to provide information that is both accurate and effective, the author does not assume any responsibility for the accuracy or use/misuse of this information.

ABOUT THE AUTHOR

My name is Travis Woods, and the poems that you are about to read are the results of both a troubled life and a redeemed soul.

I first began writing at an early age, inspired by my mother, Mrs. Marjorie Woods. Mother of eight children, all of which she shared her love with until passing at the age of 90 years old. Having been raised in a small community I always had dreams of moving out and starting my new life. This all came true at the age of 16. I graduated high school by the age of 17. I was working and had my own home, but I still helped my mother with my four younger brothers and sisters.

I always took out time to write something down that made sense to me. After serving two years in the US Army, I was shot point blank range in the head and was pronounced dead for eight minutes. After this I gave my life to God as a servant, for that I am pleased.

Today I thank God, my mother, and all of my brothers and sisters for their encouragement, and most of all, my loving wife Mrs. Sharon Woods who took the time to print and help me to finally get this to you. Thanks also to my niece Miss Ashley Fisher who helped with typing and printing this manuscript. I pray these poems will bring you comfort in times of trouble, love and peace in the middle of your storm and most of all a closer walk-in life with Our Lord and Savior Jesus Christ as your friend.

These poems are shared with you from the heart and mind of Mr. Travis Woods.

Visions
from
My Heart

TABLE OF CONTENTS

Spiritual Poems

Poems For Loved Ones and Myself

Poems for Holidays and Special Days

Spiritual

Poems

Never Had the Time

There are so many things in life that I wanted to do, but I always was too busy just trying to make it through.

I never had the time.

I was taught to give thanks to God for his mercy and grace, because one day I would have to meet him face to face.

I never had the time.

He said that he would never leave nor forsake me, but I was blinded by material things and could not see.

I never had the time.

Then one day I woke up in heaven with God looking down at me, the array of colors was so beautiful I could barely see.

I never had the time.

He said your life has been filled with envy and strife, as he opened the book of life.

You have brought upon yourself such misery and shame, and in this book, I can't find your name.

You see I never had the time.

Written 6/19/2020

Just Stand

When the world around you starts to crumble down, and discouragement says to you, turn around.

Just stand

When all your friends start pointing their fingers at you, and you're so confused until you don't know what to do.

Just stand

When old man Satan comes knocking at your door, and your heart is so hurt you can't take anymore.

Just stand

Then one day you realize that you are doing what's right, suddenly all of your troubles seem to take flight.

Just stand

Oh Lord, I thank you for your unchanging hand, because you keep giving me strength to stand.

Written 3/25/2002

Check On My Mind

When the world around you starts closing in, it's time to stop and check on the ones you call your friend.

Now things have changed from when we first began, the seriousness of life has now turned into fun.

Oh, how hard it is to live this life, especially when in my heart I was searching for a wife.

Both now I find that all my dreams are not meant to come true, I guess the real happiness of life can only be found in you.

As life goes on, we have to keep on growing, and by living a spiritual life our love will keep on flowing.

Yes, it is true that words can surely mend a heart and sometimes even comfort our mind, but there are some things in our body that say true love is what we are hoping to find.

Written 3/20/2003

3

Jesus Is the Reason Why

Let us rejoice and give God some praise, and thank him for blessing us through all of our days.

There will be gifts for children, the husband and wife, but the greatest of all is the gift of life.

We should all be proud of where we stand, as we hold on to his unchanging hand.

As God looks down on mother earth, I know he's proud of Jesus' birth.

So, I wish you happiness as these holidays pass, and remember the birth of Jesus is the reason why.

Written 3/20/2012

Thanks for Another Day

As we lay our bodies down to rest at night, we are protected by God and his holy light.

Although we might be troubled or filled with sorrow, still we have hopes of facing tomorrow.

By faith we know that everything is going to work out, because God is always with us without any doubt.

The Lord said have faith and come to me in prayer, and soon an Angel of comfort will surely be there.

God keeps giving us strength he has opened our eyes and showed us the way, so we should all give him praise and say thank you for another day.

Written 4/01/2012

Keep Your Head Up

Many times, in our lives we go through different changes, trials and tribulations, we should all be thankful to God for his patience, love and dedication.

For some of us, we've been running this race for so long, but through our fate God has always been there to keep us strong.

I'm so glad today that my eyes have been opened so that I can see, all of the blessings that the Lord keeps on giving.

Now God is pouring out his Blessing so just trust in him and let his holy spirit fill your cup, and when you are faced with obstacles you can keep your head up.

Written 4/22/2012

Hell in God's House

There's a great disturbance across the land, brothers and sisters fighting with Satan and trying to hold on to God's unchanging hand.

Even here at Greater Saint Luke, there is envy and jealousy when it's Satan we should be fighting to rebuke.

We all will have to answer for our actions, so I'm going to do my best to give God some satisfaction.

Now there is a message in what I'm trying to extend, so let's all just pray and say Amen.

Written 4/14/2012

A Shadow of Darkness

With each passing day I strive to stay ahead, hoping to find true happiness before I'm dead.

Although my eyes are open, I still can't see, because there's a dark shadow constantly following me.

I keep praying to God above, to guide me with his precious love.

Maybe there is someone out there who feels the same way too, if so, then hear my cry and tell me what to do.

Living this life is not easy, fighting the devil and serving God too.

I know that only God can bring happiness, his holy light shining brightly through this shadow of darkness.

Written 7/18/2022

A Message from the Holy Master

Please open your eyes and take a look, you'll find what you need written in my holy book.

I will release the pain of secrets you're trying to hide, and as you go through life, I will be right by your side.

As you study the Bible it will strengthen your mind, then your heart will be at peace with the joy you will find.

I will give you strength and help you stand, just have faith and hold on to my unchanging hand.

Now your heart should be filled with love and laughter, after hearing a message from the holy master.

Written 7/28/2013

9

Starting All Over Again

I realize now that the end is near, and facing reality is my greatest fear.

I have wasted too much time chasing after dreams, making my life harder; trying to swim upstream.

With nothing but love being given to me, my eyes were too busy looking to even see.

I don't know how long it will take to straighten things out, but today I surrender to God so I will make it without a doubt.

So please forgive me for my mistakes in the past, hopefully I've found my true purpose in life at last.

I only pray that God will forgive me in the end because today I am starting all over again.

Written 9/26/2013

Visions of My Mind

We take our thanks, problems and cares to the Lord each time
we pray,
And when we wake up in the morning, we fight with Satan
each and every day.

Oh, what a battle this can sometimes be, because evil
temptation can blind so that you can't see.
But I'm also thankful for God's mercy and grace; with this
we can handle all obstacles with a smile on our face.

Now we have the strength to stand, so please hold on to
God's unchanging hand.

I don't know if I'm the only one with this thought.
Or maybe it's God's way of telling us that He's so sweet and
kind, as he comes to you by the visions of my mind.

Written 11/03/2013

Thanks To You

As I stop and look back over my past, I can see where I have missed so many things while moving too fast.
Little simple things, how did I let them slip away when they were right before my eyes each and every day?

I can sometimes feel a person's heart by the expression on their face; there are signs where pain and heartache has left its traces.
There were many times when I felt lost and sometimes confused, refusing to help anyone because in my mind I was only being used.

Then one day God touched my heart and helped me to see,
He said to let go of yourself and put all of your faith in me.
Now my heart is filled with love that I'm happy to give, and I treasure the little things in life every moment that I live.
I also keep God first in everything I do, and I will forever be singing praises to your holy name.

Written 2/07/2017

Thanks To You – 2

Thank you, Lord, for this life that you have given me to live, and filling my heart with happiness and love that's free to give.

You have brought me from a mighty long way, and you continue to bless me day after day.

Today I'm proud of the things I do. I enjoy my life now, thanks to you.

So many times, I had given up on myself, and finally I realized that there was only one choice left.

I surrendered my mind, body, and soul into your hands. And now I have solid ground on which I stand.

Heavenly Father please help me to be strong, and I ask your forgiveness for everything that I have done wrong.

Now I have the strength to stand up and fight, because my eyes are open and I'm walking in your light.

I ask that it's your will Lord in everything that I do, and in my heart Lord I will forever give my thanks to you.

Written 4/12/2014

13

But God

There were times in my life when I was blind and could not see, thinking that no one else could help me.

But God

As I laid in the hospital on my deathbed, suffering from a bullet wound to the head.

But God

I have traveled so many miles across this land; sometimes things would happen that I didn't understand.

But God

Now as I go through life from day to day, I realized that there has to be someone who's leading the way.

But God

So, when Satan and different obstacles try to block my road, I know who to call and lighten my load.

But God

Now I rejoice as my heart begins to sing, because I have someone who can fix anything.

Written 8/5/2014

Please Forever e in Our Heart

You are the master who created mother earth, but still oh Lord you took out time to watch over us since our date of birth.

And by your grace and mercy we've gotten a little older, now we feel the weight of the cross that you carried on your shoulders.

And we thank you for all that you do, for giving us the strength and guidance to make it through.

You're precious, Lord, to us in so many ways, and we pray that you will be with us in all our passing days.

We love you Lord and never want to be apart, so today we say please forever be in our heart.

Written 9/15/2014

To God Up Above

I'm writing this to you and because I don't know how much time is left, I can't speak for everyone else only for myself.

I realize that I haven't lived my life the way it was meant to be, for that oh Lord, I pray you will forgive me.

Today I just want to thank you for standing by me for so very long, and please forgive me for all the things I have done wrong.

The truth is Lord I'm tired of living this way, so I hope that you will hear me Lord and help me see a better day.

I hope that my family and friends will all remember my love, I feel like soon I'll be going to God up above.

Written 12/17/2014

All Our Faith in You

In each of our lives we learn to love our children, husbands and wives.

But there also comes a time when we can't seem to go any further, that's why we have to constantly pray to one greater than any other.

The master of us all and the one we can always call.
Now most of us have tried to do things our way, and found that life gets harder with each passing day.

By living this way, we are certain to fail, but with faith the size of a mustard seed we can prevail.

So, no matter where we go or whatever we do, we will keep all our faith in you.

Written 1/04/2015

Please Break These Chains

Oh Lord with all power in your hand, please have mercy on us and give us the strength to stand.

I'm asking you to move theses clouds so the storms can cease, purify these earthly souls and give us happiness and peace.

Oh Lord please break these chains, I'm tired of losing when there is so much to gain.

Show me the way, and guide my steps as I go through the day.

Although some memories will remain, I pray that you will, please, break these chains.

Written 4/12/2015

Just Be Content

God keeps blessing us from up above, every day we're given a portion of His love. Instead of being content we constantly complain, we even run for cover when it's just a sprinkle of rain.

And we keep our hands stretched out to the sky, but when something goes wrong the first thing that we say is why? Then we start pointing our finger looking for someone to blame, with just one word from God we hold our heads down in shame.

So today let's thank God for his blessings that are heavenly sent, give him praise and just be content.

Written 6/13/2015

Just Believe

I had a dream and it came true, when I met an Angel with nothing but love shining through.

She took me by the hand and showed me the way, I learned to trust in God and always pray.

I will always cherish this memory knowing that we will never part, because now I know the purpose of giving love from the heart.

So now when I'm pressured or have a pain that I need to relieve, I just send a prayer to God and believe.

Written 6/07/2015

When Prayers Go Up
Blessings Come Down

Sometimes in life we are faced with decisions that we must make, and most of the time on our own we end up with pain and heartache.

And then we seek answers from our family or a friend, but still we're left lost or confused in the end.

So, we begin to think about what we are taught in the past. To always keep God first and put ourselves last.

And suddenly we begin to pray, now we have faith that God will show us the right way.

But soon we realize that regardless of the problem of yours or mine, along with faith there must be patience for God moves at his own pace and time.

By now we are confident that He has heard our call, and being the God that He is, He has taken care of it all.

So, hold onto your faith and let nothing turn you around, just remember when prayers go up blessings come down.

Written 7/06/2015

21

As We Grow

From our day of birth, we have experienced the pain that comes with being here on earth.

But God has been there to keep us strong, only by His grace and mercy have we lasted for so long.

His holy spirit dwells in our heart, so now it's time for us to do our part.

It's time to release the love that's hidden inside, and be a servant; rather than just go along for the ride.

Although there is pain and danger all around, God is always there to keep our feet on solid ground.

So, let's take out this time to let our true love flow, and get closer to God every day as we grow.

Written 8/16/2015

Blinded By Confusion

With each passing day a line of confusion comes our way,
this line causes us confusion and we forget who is blessing us
day by day.

Let us stop and take time out, so we can give God the praise
and see what true love is all about.

We depend on God with His blessing to fulfill and that He
asks of us to just do his will.

Although living this life is not easy to do, just have faith in
God he will surely be there for you.

Now I'm not where I would like to be, but I know that my
God is the One who's leading me. If you feel the same way
too, then give God some praise and watch what he will do.

Jesus died upon the cross, so please live your life so that his
was not a loss.

Written 9/15/2015

This Man 1 Had Met

He came to me out of the blue, and said I see that it's time to talk to you.

I see that old Satan had a hold on you, but if you will follow my path, I will help you make it through.

I couldn't believe this; it all seemed like a dream, but I stayed there as tears began flowing like water in a stream.

Again, he spoke and said why live your life filled with heartache and pain: when you could be happy with me and have so much to gain?

When the tears stopped, I could see this man standing over me as I looked up from my bending knee.

Now I look forward to a better day, thanks to this man who is leading the way.

Written 1/07/2016

Where Is Your Faith?

We have all been blessed by God above, with each passing day we receive a touch of his precious love.

Where is your faith?

But this love goes even further, it is meant to be given back to God, ourselves, and also our sisters and brothers.

Where is your faith?

As Christians we walk in God's holy light, our heart should be grounded and compelled to do what's right.

Where is your faith?

Today Greater Saint Luke, let us rejoice because it's Satan whom we rebuke.
Let's come together and make a stand, have faith in God and hold on to his unchanging hand.

Where is your faith?

Written 7/14/2016

Lost and Confused

I can see the prodigal son as he traveled out into a distant land, having a good time while wasting his money and feeding the Devil's hand.

Then one day after all his money was gone, he looked around for a friend, but found out he was all alone.

Oh, what a lonely feeling this must have been, to be all alone and trapped in a world of sin.

While thinking he was by himself, he realized that he had one friend left.

So, on his knees he decided to fall and God was right there and heard his call.

God gave him strength to see another day, and showed him the way home and led him all the way.

I know the prodigal son and realize how hard life can be, because the prodigal son that I'm speaking of is me.

After being trapped in sin, used and abused, God took my hand because he knew that I was tired of being lost and confused.

Written 9/08/2016

My Angel of Love

Oh, Angel of Love come down and take me on a flight, high above the clouds where darkness never hides the light.

Give me wings so that I can fly along by your side, and let your Holy Spirit be my guide.

The door to my heart is open wide, waiting for you to come and take me for a ride.

I can feel the warmth of your loving care and my heart is filled with love that I need to share.

So today I'm asking God above, to send me down to my Angel of Love.

Written 2/14/2017

I'm Still with You

Don't let your hearts be filled with pain and sorrow, just thank God for today but dream about tomorrow.

My dreams have finally come true; although I'm standing here with God my love is still with you.

So, hold onto it and bury it deep in your heart, because what God has joined together no one can take it apart.

Now I have a friend who has given me a life that will never end.

I have been blessed and forgiven for my past; I give God praise constantly because I found peace at last.

Just remember no matter where you go or what you do, my love is always there and I'm still with you.

Written 4/17/2017

Poems For Loved Ones and Myself

We Love You Mother

You carried us for nine months and then gave birth; you welcomed us with open arms as we entered onto Mother Earth.

Through our blurry eyes we could see, this is the way that God wanted life to be.

You were always there showing us guidance and love, then you took out time to tell us about God and Heaven above.

Surrounded by love we were well on our way, as you reminded us to always pray.

As time passed on and we began to get older, we started to feel the weight of this old world upon our shoulders.

Sometimes we have doubts about going any further, then we found strength in God and you, our mother.

Whose love is everlasting and like no other, we love you always and forever, Mother.

Written 5/12/2019

Our Pastor

Today we're giving honor to a lady who has stepped up to the plate, sharing the word of God with love and guidance that we all appreciate.

I have watched her grow down through the years, facing her challenges without any fears.

As a leader she checks to make sure that everything is done right, always there to help anyone whether it is day or night.

When she stands behind the altar to preach the word, you can feel the Holy Spirit's touch so you'll remember what you heard.

I am so proud today being a member of NCC, I feel like God placed you where he wants you to be.

I believe that I can speak for all the members when I say that here at in NCC serving God has become our main factor, thanks to the guidance of Minister Wanda Bullock, our pastor.

Written 7/06/2019

To the Woods Family

Love and laughter; togetherness that we should all be after.

We have shared this love down through the years, and it has grown even stronger through the pain and the tears.

We are here today by God's mercy and grace, and I hope that you will share your love as we greet each other face to face.

We show our remembrance of Jesus Christ each time we have communion, so I pray that in your heart you will never forget this family reunion.

We all love each other this you should know, so please take this time out to let your love flow.

Written 4/17/2019

I Will Survive

This is dedicated to a man who has traveled around the world; he goes by the name of Pastor Gerald.

Now he spends his time as a director of peoples' paths, sharing his knowledge and understanding.

Oh, what a blessing this has been for me, he has helped me to open my eyes and now I can see.

These words are more precious than diamonds and pearls; they came to me along this love and care from Pastor Gerald.

Thank you for your time and dedication.

Written 5/14/2017

Dedicated to Mr. Royce

Early this morning I heard a voice, it caught my attention; it was my counselor, Mr. Royce.

Then I began to wonder in the back of my mind, because it seemed as if he was soul searching; I wonder what will he find?

His words touched deep, I found it easy to resist the sleep.

It's almost like magic, it took me through a loop, this man is getting a point across to this wild and crazy group.

Gifting us peace and confidence with the knowledge in his head, showing us a way of life before we end up dead.

I thank God today for this man, who gave us the tools to help us stand.

Thank you!

Written 11/12/2016

Music to Our Ears

Today we give thanks to three people for their hard work and dedication, as the use of their talents are shared with us, helping us to praise God as we go through our many situations.

To Sister Karen Flenroy, we thank you for your heavenly voice as you sing to our Holy Father. Thank you for making the right choice.

To Bro. Alan, we thank you for your outstanding sound, and bringing joy to us all with every beat in every pound.

To Sis. Wilma Franks, we thank you for being all that you can be, and the peace that you bring with the stroke of the piano keys.

To you all, your music has helped us through happiness, heartache, pain and tears.

May God bless you as you continue to bring music to our ears.

Written 11/12/2012

Love

Love has been given to us all from the start, now it's time for us to do our part.

Open your heart and let love flow, don't be afraid to let your feelings show.

Remove the dark clouds so that God's light can shine, allowing the Holy Spirit to unite your heart with mine.

Today let's give thanks to God above, for his patience, understanding, and most of all for His precious love.

Written 2/24/2015

We Are Not Alone

As we go through our lives from day to day, we are sometimes face to face with different obstacle in our way.

So, we lift our heads up to the sky praying that you Oh Lord will give us the strength to get by.

By our faith you have helped us to stand, so we surrender ourselves unto you Oh Lord assured that we are in the best hands.

Although this pain in our hearts may cause tears to fall, in the name of Jesus it's your holy name that we call.

Although one of your angels has been called home to rest, we can still find a little peace because only you, Lord, knows what is best.

Even with pain that aches down to our bones, we thank you Lord for showing us that we are not alone.

Written 1/2/2022

The Emptiness Inside

With each passing day, we all pray for a spark of happiness to come our way. But when loneliness is all, we find, oh, what a strain this puts on our mind.

Surely this is not the way our lives should be, when all around us there is so much beauty and love for our eyes to see.

But loneliness is so very hard to hide, especially when we have to deal with this constant emptiness inside.

Our hunger for happiness has never been so strong, and we look back on life and wonder where did we go wrong?

Why is there so much heartache and pain, or have we been relaxing in the sun too long and now it's our time to stand alone in the rain.

I pray that the Holy Spirit will find a place in my heart to reside and help me remove the emptiness inside.

Written 2/02/2022

Just Hold On

When we choose to walk down the path of the straight and narrow road, we sometimes find that our strength comes through faith which helps us to carry the weight of this world's heavy load.

Although it's true that our help comes from above, we enjoy life better as we say no to hatred and try sharing a little love.

And not everyone is willing to accept what we have to offer, but we find peace when we kneel down and pray before the altar.

Every day we have decisions we must make, but only God knows how much we can take.

We all know that one day this life will come to an end, so we should be building a relationship with our Lord and Savior as our friend.

Yes, our time is coming and no one knows how long, so let's keep our faith in God and just hold on.

Written 8/11/2016

Brother to Brother

He lived a lifetime doing things the best he could and shared a love with others the way God would.

With each passing day, he said just hold on, the Lord will make a way.

The bond with his family was great as any other, but as for me it was the greatest because he was also my brother.

His spirit keeps saying wipe the tears from your eyes so that you can see, God has always told us that is the way our lives will be.

But don't, because God has opened the doors of heaven, send for me, instead, thank the Lord above for allowing us this time with Andrew P. Woods, whom we will always love.

Written 8/24/2014

41

An Angel of Love

Dedicated to Margaret Dick

Into our lives she came, filling our hearts with happiness with just the mention of her name.

Always willing to help whenever she could, loving and raising her children the way only an angel would.

She passed this love onto her grands and great grands down the line, even to other families like yours and mine.

I pray that we cherish our memories as they cross our mind, and remember the love Margaret shared was one-of-a-kind.

Today we won't say goodbye, just farewell, because when we think about the love, we have a story to tell.

So let us give thanks to God above, for the time that we spent with Mrs. Margaret who was truly an Angel of Love.

Written 8/06/2020

My Race Has Been Run

Dedicated to my Brother Wesley Thomas

Early this morning before the sun could rise, I was greeted by an Angel right before my eyes.

Your race is over and it's time to go home, there's a new family waiting to welcome you because this is where you belong.

Now when I meet my father, I wonder what he would say, I know that I'm not perfect and made mistakes along the way,

I have lots of friends and lived life the best I could, doing things righteously, giving praise to God the way that I should.

I know that God is merciful and brings out the goodness in me but until this day is over there is no guarantee.

Right now, I wish that I could live my life all over again, I'm sure that God's book of life would have only a few marks of sin.

But today I have to fess up to the works I've done, I put my trust in God because I know that this battle has been won.

Written 3/05/2010

Happy Birthday My Son

Well, here you are at the age of 56, and now you have a spiritual family who has welcomed you into their mix.

Singing and praising our father above, with arms wide open and sharing their love.

You have gone through heartaches, misery and pain, then you called on the Lord so he delivered you from the rain.

Now the way you live is up to you, but God has shown you a way of happiness without doing the things that you're used to.

Very few people have the pleasure of getting to meet the maker, and then enjoy the gift of love thereafter.

But here you stand, as proof of miracles that happen while holding on to God's unchanging hand.

So please continue to live righteously and enjoy getting old, but always remember that God is in control.

He's always there to help you along the way, that's why you should rejoice and be happy as you celebrate this 56th birthday.

Written 3/28/2010

A Touch of Love

I met a lady whose love has touched my heart, gifting happiness and I pray we will never part.

She has opened my eyes and helped me to see, the true love of God and what he wants us to be.

Always respect our father and mother, the Bible says for us all to love one another.

Now I will share this love for as long as I live, and thanks to God and his angels, I have more to give.

Oh, how happy this makes me feel, to meet someone so young but most of all who's for real.

Today I give thanks to God above, for just allowing me to feel his precious touch of love.

Written 4/08/2021

Reaching Out for Love

Day by day I strive to stay ahead, hoping to find true happiness before they pronounce me dead.

So many times, I've put my love on the line, only to hurt so badly until I couldn't believe this was mine.

Although I have no regrets of the time that I have spent, because the love I give is heavenly sent.

As long as I have life, this love continuously flows, when this search for happiness will end God only knows.

Maybe there's someone out there who feels the same way too, if so, then please hear my cry and tell me what to do.

As for me I'm praying to God above, to please help me to be strong while reaching out for love.

Written 2/08/2019

Happy Father's Day

Deep down inside the soul of my mind, I can hear the cry of a lonely man reaching out for serenity that he cannot find.

Tormented by memories of the past, wishing this would all end; wondering how long he can last.

Surrounded by a world of sin, wishing he had the opportunity to live his life over again.

Finally, one night in the middle of a prayer, he heard a voice saying *I will always be there.*

By his faith he realized that no longer had to live in sin, by the mercy and grace of God, he had been born again.

Now there's a little happiness from day to day, because he's trusting God to lead the way.

Written 6/20/2016

To All My Children

After doing so much wrong we finally decided to do what's right, realized we are being led by God's holy and guiding light.

There is peace between the husband and wife, as we go through the days of life.

But the devil comes around to try and end our happiness; temptation to let us know that we live on the edge of darkness.

Keep your eyes open and listen for God's sounds, because he talks to us daily as the world spins round.

Now that he's got your attention share the love that's free to give, and always remember we only have one life to live.

Written 10/21/2013

God's Creation

We have been chosen to live on this precious land, and everywhere we look we can see the works of God Almighty's hand.

As we embrace the beauty that's all around, we can give praise to God without making a sound.

But life is not all about what we see; one of our greatest services is sharing the true love that is within you and me.

Although I realize that this is not always easy to do, just remember that God is watching you too.

Today I pray that there be peace in all nations, as we give all the praise to God and God's creations.

Written 4/12/2018

Judgment Day

While riding alone one night in the car, I happen to notice a falling star.

I hear a soft and sweet sound, seeing that it's just another lost soul that has been cast down.

They have made the trip to see the Master and found out that their life has been a disaster.

Now there's no chance to live again, they're doomed forever in a world of sin.

To live a life without love is a price that no one wants to pay, to be cast down from Heaven on judgment day.

Written 12/12/2017

To All God's Children

He came into this world as a mystery; by fulfilling his purpose he claimed victory.

There were those who wanted to kill him from his day of birth, although through his works the followers cried as he was lifted from Mother Earth.

His life was dedicated to save God's children from sin, he laid down his life and his father raised him up again.

Some people asked what kind of man could this be, who gave his life so that others could one day be free.

I pray that we will all read and remember the words that he had to say, because his Holy Spirit leads us day by day.

So, let's give him the praise and glory, and live our lives based on his story.

Jesus died upon the cross; live your life righteously so his was not a loss.

Written 12/24/2017

In the Shadow of Your Love

We go through our lives from day to day, leaning and depending on God to lead the way.

Oh, how wonderful this life can be, walking in God's Holy Spirit with our eyes open so we can see.

Although living this life is not always easy to do, but there is peace knowing that God is watching over me and you.

By faith we continue to be strong, always praying for forgiveness for the things we've done wrong.

Singing and giving praise to his holy name, as we walk proudly and not in shame.

Today we give thanks to you, God above, as we continue to walk boldly in the shadow of your love.

Written 2/14/2018

On the Road to Heaven

For years I have traveled down this road and now realize that this is too heavy a load.

As time passed by, I began to think my life could be over in just one blink.

My conscience told me it's time to take the step; surrender to God and ask for help.

I kneeled down and began to pray, asked God to take control and lead the way.

Give me the strength to stand up and fight, dwell in this earthly frame so that my light may shine bright.

Today I thank God for his precious love, as he watches over us all from Heaven above.

Written 7/14/2020

Take that Step Today

As we go through life from day to day, we will have to face stumbling blocks along the way.

No one can choose your mountain or tell you when to climb, it's yours alone to challenge at your own pace and time.

No one knows the time or the hour, only God above has the power.

So maybe it's time to take this step today, your burdens will be light if you follow the things he says.

God said have faith in me and I will set you free, beware of false prophets, because there is none greater than me.

Hold on to my unchanging hand, and I will place your feet on a solid rock and then you will understand.

There is nothing that I can't do, and I will never leave nor forsake you.

If you will take one step, I will take two, take heed to what I say I might need your time, so take that step today.

Written 8/12/2019

Your Mercy and Grace

We have come this far by faith, leaning and depending on God above, being blessed each day with a touch of His precious love.

Today we give God all the glory and praise, as we thank him for guiding and protecting us in so many ways.

God blessed Greater Saint Luke with his temple, built on solid rock on which it will stand and a congregation who worships and praises Him hand in hand.

Living this life is not always easy to do, but by faith and prayer we are making it through.

We look forward to that day when we may see the beauty of that heavenly place, when we can rejoice with the angels as we thank you Lord for your mercy and grace.

Written 8/18/2019

Here Today and Gone Tomorrow

When we stop and look around, we see that some of our family and friends have been returned to rest in the ground.

In the moment our hearts are filled with pain as the tears flow down our face like rain.

But through faith we go on with our lives, sharing love with our friends, children, husbands and wives.

This can sometimes be hard to do, when we still have sadness and want to be happy too.

So, we lift up our head, have faith in the living God and not the dead.

Please don't waste your time wrestling your mind.

Leave your heart with pain and sorrow and remember that we are here today and gone tomorrow.

Written 9/15/2019

It's Time to Surrender

As we wake up each day we are faced with trials and tribulations; don't feel bad this is happening all across the nation.

Very often we can feel abandoned and all alone, with our hearts reaching out for this place where our soul belongs.

Here we stand heartbroken, lost, and confused, tired of sharing our love yet feeling used and abused.

Then we ask ourselves where did we go wrong, we have a talk with God we know that his answer won't take long.

Maybe we haven't been faithful to God and have only been a pretender, now that we have our answer let's get together because it's simply time to surrender.

Written 9/18/2019

God is Watching Over Me

While sitting here with my eyes open wide, filled with serenity and happiness inside.

I begin to think about the wonders of His love, and how we all have been blessed by God up above.

There were so many things running through my mind, I wondered if God was checking my past and what would he find?

Suddenly a soft voice said to me, *the pathway of your life has already been reviewed by me,*

I knew then that I had done many things knowing God wouldn't agree.

Now was the time to be true to God and allow my eyes to open so that I can see, because I realize now that God is watching over me.

Written 10/22/2019

God Heard My Prayers

There are times in our lives when trouble tries to bring us down, turning most of our smiles into a frown.

Through this so many of us lose faith and feel abandoned or lost, but we have to remember that day on Calvary when Jesus paid the cost.

Jesus never said there will be no heartache or pain, but he did say that he will always be there through the storm and the rain.

So down on our knees we fall, and it's his holy name that we call.

Saying Lord, Lord please have mercy on me, come take away this darkness so that a Sinner will be able to see.

Soon an Angel of Comfort is sent down from above, a symbol of God's precious love. It's true that God is always there, I'm a living witness because God heard my prayer.

Written 2/13/2021

A Spiritual Heart

As humans we rely on our heart to give its constant beat, but, in reality, without God in our lives the heart is incomplete.

Because it is God and God alone who supplies us with the strength that lies within our bones.

Our hearts not only supply blood but also love. Our love is to be shared by all mankind from God above for so many people this can be hard to do, and that decision is up to you.

A spiritual love goes deeper down into our soul, by our faith in God this is given freely each day as our lives unfold.

We are always connected to God with a love that would never part, because we have chosen to live our lives faithfully sharing true love from a spiritual heart.

Written 2/27/2021

Are You Ready to Meet Me?

I have watched over you every day since your day of birth, I gave you commandments to direct your path while here on Earth.

I gave you a heart and filled it with love, and even made room for you in Heaven above.

Now you have brought all of this to shame, and both day and night you keep calling out my name.

Saying Lord, Lord please have mercy and save me. This is not the way I want my life to be.

Although I have forgiven you over and over again, you say thank you Lord and return to doing wrong and sin.

You have a home in Heaven where you are meant to be, so I ask you today, are you ready to meet me?

Written 3/12/2021

To Take Us for a Ride

When we stop and look back at all the things that we have been through, we often think of our parents who taught us all that they knew.

Things like always pray and do your best, keep your faith in God and he will handle the rest.

As you travel down life's highways there will be times when trials and tribulations will try and block your road, but remember that Jesus our Lord and Savior is always there and will help to carry your load.

At this point in life your lights should be shining a little brighter, and the weight on your shoulders should be a little lighter.

So, go on my child and let your light shine and don't be afraid to share the love that was given to your heart and mine.

Yes, we have many memories of our past, and it seems like this time has gone by too fast.

But don't be discouraged, our greatest joy is on the other side. On that glorious day when our Lord and Savior comes down to take us for a ride.

Written 4/20/2021

God is Still on the Throne

As I go through my life from day to day, I have no idea about the troubles that are coming my way.

I hold on to my faith in One who has all power, realizing that at any time I could be living my last hour.

And suddenly it hits, it seemed as though I had fallen into a deep, deep pit.

As I struggled to rise from my bed, there were many thoughts running through my head.

Why is my body feeling so tired? Has my time on earth just expired?

Maybe I will eat but that's a waste, because not only could I not smell I had also lost my taste.

So off to the doctor I go, hoping for a different answer from what I already know.

They say, *yes Mr. Woods it's true, the deadly virus has caught up with you.*

And my first thought was that I serve a God with the power to do all my healing, who can take away this pain and misery that I'm feeling.

I kneeled down and began to pray, assured that a touch of his healing was coming my way.

I heard a voice saying I hear your prayer, I am with you, you are never alone; God is still on the throne.

Written 8/07/2021

Time is Running Out

When we stop today and look all around, we see storms, diseases and deaths occurring in almost every town.

People keep moving from here to there, and find the same thing is happening everywhere.

While hospital beds are being filled to the max, some of us are only thinking about their next stimulus check or waiting on their income tax period.

But as life goes on and time keeps passing by, maybe we should lift our heads and start looking up to the sky.

As we start praying continuously to God above, and ask for his protection, mercy, and grace with a touch of his precious love.

Maybe then our eyes will open to see that our Lord and Savior is coming back one day for you and me.

The Devil, yes, it's true our final day on earth is coming without a doubt, so please draw closer to our savior, because our time is running out.

Written 9/12/2021

This Man Named Jesus

He came into this world in the form of man, because his father knew that if anyone could save His people; His son can.

As Jesus traveled across this land, he was victorious over many kings and never raised his hand.

His word was shared in many nations, everywhere he went people gathered in what we call congregations.

Many times, his life was in danger, because some were afraid and confused by the powerful words they heard from this complete stranger.

Somewhere healed by faith and some by his touch, never before had they seen one man who could do so much.

Even his disciples' hearts and minds were changed by his words and what they believed, but Jesus knew that by one of his own one day he would be deceived.

Here we are today with presidents, governors, policemen and others.

But none would willingly give their life to save us, no there is no one like this man named Jesus.

Written 12/05/2021

Remember Me

As we stop and look back over our lives, we should all say thank to the One who has kept us and helped us to survive.

Today we give God and our Lord and Savior Jesus Christ all of the glory as we live our life learning from the holy words of his story.

Being led by his Holy Spirit, praising daily for guidance and strength to continue our walk in it.

We come to you today, oh Lord, not with fashion or fame, we come giving praise unto your holy name.

Thanking you for teaching us and helping us each day, and opening our ears to hear your voice saying to always Remember Me.

Written 1/09/2022

Hold On

Although our stay on Earth may only last for a little while, and by keeping our faith in God we can face our trouble with a smile.

We don't have to live our lives drowning in heartache and sorrow with only a hope for tomorrow.

As Christians the Holy Spirit is always there, deep down inside so if we just hold onto our fate, we can endure this bumpy ride.

Even though the roads of life can sometimes get rough, only God above can stop it and say that's enough.

Satan is always busy trying to manipulate our minds, but a sincere prayer to God brings the greatest peace that we can find.

Let's not spend our days moaning and groaning, just remember that weeping may endure for a night but joy comes in the morning.

Written 1/17/2022

The Father of Time

Oh, Heavenly Father, we give you all the glory and praise as we come to you for strength and guidance to be obedient to your Word and your ways.

We pray for your shelter from the storm of this virus as it passes by.

Realizing that all of our help comes from you, oh Lord, high above the sky.

By our faith we will continue to hold on, resting assured that one day you will lead us home.

In that last moment of life, rather it is yours or mine, may our hearts be at peace when we meet the Father of Time.

Written 1/22/2022

Living By God's Words

My mother always told me to be careful about the things you say, if not they may come back to haunt you one day.

As Christians, the words that we give should be an example of the love we receive and they are also a statement of who we are and what we believe.

Although no one among us is perfect, life can be hard sometimes while serving God and fighting with the Devil too.

But we can always find strength when we reach deep down in our souls, there we will find all the power that we need; all we have to do is surrender and allow God's Holy Spirit to take control.

This may not be for everyone maybe it's only for myself, but there are so many things in my past that I'm glad I left.

Today I pray God will strengthen my heart and my mind, help me to comprehend the holy words that I've heard as I continue to live by God's words.

Written 1/02/2022

A New Beginning

As we look around today, we can see the trees start to bud and flowers show signs of life, even the birds as they sing, truly a sign of an oncoming spring.

When we commit our lives to our Lord Savior Jesus Christ, things begin to change compared to our old way of living and this can sometimes feel strange.

We began to feel and see the beauty of sharing love, joy and happiness from our hearts as we begin the fulfillment of our purpose. As Christians we experience a peace that we pray will never depart.

We can feel the strength that comes with the unity that has developed our Christian family and our church.

As we look back at our lives, finally, we have a portion of peace, no longer do we have to wonder and search.

Remember, Jesus died upon the cross, so please live your life righteously so that his was not a loss.

When our life here on earth comes to an end, we can face it with confidence and faith knowing that it's really a new beginning.

Written 3/06/2022

Poems for Holidays and Special Days

It's the Christmas Season

Yes, it's that golden time of the year, the sounds of Christmas carols and Jingle Bells is all we hear.

Now it's time to take a pause; everyone is looking for Santa Claus.

But we have to think about the life we live, have we been sharing all the love we can give?

If it's really in Santa Claus and Christ we believe, then we already know there is no greater gift to receive.

So let us give thanks to the birth of Christ, who died on Calvary and paid the price.

Let us be happy and enjoy this Christmas season, but please don't forget that Christ is the reason.

Written 12/25/2013

Christmas Day

Fill your hearts with cheer, it's the golden time of year.

Lift your heads up to the sky, and watch for Santa's sleigh to pass by.

Prepare your eyes for what you might see, the gifts that are coming to you and me

I can see a light that's bright as day, because there are angels pulling his sleigh.

Now I can pray that you all have been obedient and nice, because the sleighs are being guided by Jesus Christ.

Let us rejoice as he comes our way, while we celebrate his birth on Christmas Day.

Written 12/25/2002

Thanksgiving

As we sit down with our family and friends to celebrate, we should all stop and think about the real things we should appreciate.

Will it be the material things we may possess, or the joy we feel through our love and happiness?

Remember God wants us all to be happy in life and to share love with our friends, children, husband and wife.

But all of these things only come by keeping our heart and eyes on the star, the star that watches over us and has brought us to where we are.

So, for myself, today, I give thanks to our Lord and Savior Jesus Christ and our Heavenly Father up above, who has forgiven all my sins and leads me through life with his mercy, grace and a touch of his precious love.

Yes, I'm thankful for this life I am living, and I wish you all a very happy and safe Thanksgiving.

Written 11/21/2021

Black History

Today we take a look back to those who were first to stand and were always there to lend a helping hand.

We begin with Miss Frances Harper, born free in Baltimore. She was poet, abolitionist, teacher, writer, and a public speaker.

She helped slaves make their way along the Underground Railroad to Canada; she formed the first national association of colored women in 1894.

Born 1825 through 1977, Miss Mary Fields, known as Stagecoach Mary at age 63 was the first black woman to work for the US Postal Service. If the snow was too deep for her horse, she carried sacks on her shoulders.

Phyllis Wheatley born 1753 in West Africa sold into slavery learned to read and write by the age of nine and became the first black woman to publish a book of poetry. After reading one of her poems, President George Washington requested to meet with her in 1776.

Denmark Carpenter born 1767 as a slave, but won a lottery and bought his freedom, yet unable to buy his wife and children a bed. He founded the first African Methodist Episcopal Church but in 1800 he and five others were found guilty of planning slave revolt and hung in 1822.

Written 2/01/2022

Our Black History

Most of our grandparents spent their entire lives working as slaves, and their only peace came by praying or when they were laid down in their graves.

They were used, abused and brought to shame; they didn't even have the right to choose their own name.

On March 11, 1820 Miss Harriet Tubman was born. In 1863 she was a scout for the union commanders, she helped liberate enslaved people for the first black union regiment. She was the conductor of the Underground Railroad. In her words, "I never ran my train off the track and I never lost a passenger". She rescued seventy people during thirteen trips to Maryland.

Rosa Parks was 42 years old when she refused to sit at the back of a bus; this has paved the way for many of us.

So, yes, we have been beat down, but today we are standing tall.

In 2009, along came our first black president, Mr. Obama and he was making the calls. Although there are many things in our lives that are still a mystery, I'm so thankful to those who fought and made our black history.

Written 2/06/2022

In Remembrance of Black History

We are free at last:

In the world today let us take time out to think about someone other than ourselves, because without our black history what would we have left?

Most of our great grandparents spent their entire lives working as slaves and only found peace when they were laid down in their grave.

They were used, abused, and brought to shame, and they didn't even have the right to choose their own name.

But down through the years after plenty of hurt, heartache and tears, we are still there standing tall. In 2009, we even had a black president and he was making the calls.

I hope that you've heard something today that's worthy of your time.

As for me, your participation and presence are reward enough in my mind.

Today, as you look back at our past, remember Dr. Martin Luther King Jr. who said "FREE AT LAST, FREE AT LAST, THANK GOD ALMIGHTY WE ARE FREE AT LAST!"

Written 2/22/2019

A Few Black Leaders

They who finally reached their goal and are now a part of history as their stories are being told.

Miss Shirley Chisholm born 1924, died 2005. During the racially contentious period of the late 60s, she became the first black woman elected to Congress.

Her slogan was unbought and unbossed, a tribute was made to her recently by Senator Kamala Harris.

Mr. Bayard Rustin 1912 to 1987, a gay man and smart, he was the brain who organized and strategized the march on Washington for Dr. Martin Luther King Jr.

Before Miss Rosa Parks, there was a 15-year-old girl named Miss Claudette Colvin who in 1939 chose not to sit at the back of a bus and became the first woman to be arrested for her resistance.

Miss Bessie Coleman, who lived from 1892 to 1926 was the first black licensed pilot in the world but wasn't recognized until after her death.

Although there is still so much more to be done, can we say that we have come a long way from our past.

Written 2/02/2022

Made in the USA
Middletown, DE
05 November 2022